"More than mere words…this rare poetry creates an experience that takes one on life's journey as a metaphor…
Judy Butzine, Founder Cultural Arts Coalition

"Holly's passion for transparency is intuitive, perceptive, raw. Thank you. I emerged a different person."
Raleigh R. Pinskey, Author, Speaker, Actress.

"Soul of A Woman… is an inspiring and spirit-soaring collection of poems that will heal your soul and accelerate your passion for what it is to be human."
Jerrie Ueberle Founder, Global Interactions and the World Academy for the Future of Women

"Potent, bite-sized poems, represent the purest definition of poetry; the fewest words, in the perfect order."
Viko Nikci, Director, Writer

"Art made visible; this poetry evoked images and feelings that took me deeper into words that then became drops in the pond of my mind and their ripples, my own.
Renee Morgan Brooks International Motivational Singer, Actor

"I love the images that you paint with your words and I am so impressed by your mastery of images and the way you evoke so many deep thoughts and feelings."
Aleksandar Saša Tešanović, Artist

Dedication

For my children
Hope, Nicole, Cody and Adriana
My granddaughters Ayla, Gaia, Amara
And all who follow…

Acknowledgements

To Dr. Ribhi M. Kalla, Teacher, Ageless Wisdom Teachings, whose guidance informs wisdom in the passion of my poetry.

To Marjory Englehorn for inspiring greatness in everyone and for gifting me with a lifetime of friendship.

To all my family and family of friends, without whose love and support this work may never have met a bookshelf. I express my deepest gratitude.

To my Editor, Heinz Kagerer and his wife Margit whose sense of precision and artistic guidance sustained my focus.

To Geronimo Rios of Pomegranate Press for creating the visual expression of my work.

Preface to Poetry

This collection expresses the soulful musings of a single, solitary woman, uncensored.

Contained within are poetic narratives and transcendent chronicles composed of hopes - dreams, success - failure, romance - loss, social misgivings and observations of future possibilities for our fragile world.

Gratitude for the endless rhythm and tempo of this epoch journey we call life, lies at the heart of this collection. Lying words like stepping stones, on barely discernable ancient paths that collectively reflect a universal mosaic, is my offering to you.

Since childhood, it has been my practice to intentionally gather and organize impressions on many levels and dimensions. My poem "Intuition" describes an aspect of myself I could not comprehend - until I began to write.

Within a week of my mother's passing in 2010, I became profoundly aware that a powerful element of her life force had moved into me. I had no idea at the time how this could be possible, much less how her energy would reorganize and transform my creative spirit.

She was not an artist or a writer and I would not describe her as an activist. The only book she left of interest was a collection titled *"Prose and Poetry of the World"* [1941, L.W. Singer publisher]. Classics by Titus Livius, Henrik Ibsen, Euripides, Plato and the translation of "Arabian Night's" by Lane, still cherish her bookmarks.

Before I began this collection I'd only penned five poems, they are *"The Maiden, Edges, Balance, Intuition, and Synergy"*.

Deconstructing my life through radical action and thoughtful reflection ultimately provided the answer to a universal human question that plagued my quiet moments. *"What is MINE to do?"*

I waited. *"Deconstruction"* was the first of 45 poems written in three days, initially released as a Limited Edition titled *"Spring Journey, Footsteps for Love and Life."* The final collection *"Soul of A Woman"* combines the enclosed 111 poems, written over a year.

Provocative by nature, reflectively personal, often simultaneously universal is the mystery of poetry. The gift is delivered when we the reader, allow ourselves to be captivated by the journey long enough to discover the key and unlock our own hidden gate.

To the degree we submit to the path of surrender, we merge with the spirit of beauty that guides all artists; conveying a new found awareness to our total being…ultimately birthing the artist within. This is the alchemy of art, the transformative power that exists only when Human potential embraces hopeful creativity.

When asked, about my writing experience, I describe *"An intimate flow of sensual energy enticing me to capture its spirit."* It has been my great privilege to comply. If any poem touches you to any meaningful degree, I remain eternally grateful…

Yours,

Journey in Love

Journey in Life

Journey in Love

THE MAIDEN

In my memory

A mischievous maiden plays

Unaffected by the shifting sands

Of each glowing moment

Impatiently, she practices the dance of life

Joyfully creating her mood

Around her swirls the space of ages

Within her lives the future

2

WOMAN

Willing

Waiting to breathe

Standing and learning

Watching and knowing

Still and wise

Challenging and mysterious

Empty and full

Full and empty

Ever

Enough

3

FIND YOUR VOICE

You have no choice

Our silent consent

We must repent

Find Your Voice

You have no choice

Restore your power

For every tomorrow

4

MOTHERHOOD

Tempest portends unknown heritage

Winks blink

Blind my stoic stare

Silence is repealed

Tranquility is transformed

Movement

Rushing

Space divided

Then ages smile on ages for ages

Deep hearts

Grow together

Eternal friends

5

HOPE

Defining the ages we agree

Hope was always meant to be

Where would the obvious find refuge

Silently watching for the obtuse to retreat

Hope waits

Beneath shattered wings, conventional myth regroups

Solitary senseless systems

Repent

While Hope waits

Germinating

Empowering

Creating

Teaching

Responding

Forgiving

6

DAUGHTERS

Spectacular

Love bubbles to life

Waddles, toddles and giggles

She grows

Stumbling into perfection

An enigma of charm

She grew

Perfectly poised

Proudly, positively, passionate

Dawn breaks; she's a woman now

Adopted by a passively hysterical world

She embraces her destiny

Knowing

The mystery will grow deeper

Her love will grow stronger

Time will forgive her

Life will never abandon her

B-DAY BLISS

Birthdays in the middle years

Bring magic to the mark

Song and yarn of yesteryear

Slowly now embark

Finer resolutions golden

Witness in your heart

Weave a path, steal a laugh

Cast your dreams upstream ...

Sweetness in the present dream

Creates from worlds unseen

GRAND

Beyond parenthood lies an epoch extraordinaire

We thought parenting would bear our reflection

Rarely it delivered unscathed perfection

Devoted

Distracted

Committed

Inexperienced

Parents discover

The sweetest ovation in the next generation

Unrelenting love

Relevance

Patently

Grand

9

GODDESS

Transformational by nature

Irreverent by design

Sacred birthright

Vulnerable

Sensitive

Powerful

She nurtures the poor in spirit

Strengthens hearts that beat for life

Disavowing deception will scar her

If she's your sister you may mock her

If she's your daughter you may destroy her

If she's your wife she may leave you

If she's your Lover

Protect her

10

SPICE OF LIFE

We created a dream today
Hung the walls, laid down spice

Made a new home to more than suffice
Grow up a family loving and nice

Sheer effervescence any cost any price
Pregnant persuasion insight or advice

Will she be brilliant will she be bold
Will she retain force of habit foretold

Can one woman end the loss, steer off blight
Stand with conviction, rally our might

Once when we wandered
Somehow we knew
As women before us
We beckon what's true

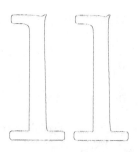

MRS E

If ever lived true elegance
If ever lived a joy
If ever lived compassion
The sun she did employ

Her smile could light a candle
Her heart could raise the dead
Her redwood graced a handle
Laughter sang within her head

No matter your apparent merit
Despite your anxious state
She saw through your disguises
Your delusions soon abate

Our grateful measure wonders
What gifts we might return
Show honor to the fallen
Generous spirits eternal tune

12

DEIRDRE O'CONNELL

Delicate memories

Expand to vistas

Scenes silently align

A pattern of genius emerged

Her name was Deirdre

Passionate for a deep life

Dramatic brilliance beckoned

Submerged in chaos

She embraced the mystery

Explore interpret personify teach

We called her Doc

Imbued with delicate power

She moved between shadows as a doe in snow

Translating the unsaid littered between lines

She created a troupe

Deposited a legacy

Irreplaceable

Ever faithful

Ever grateful

Ever friends

13

CODY

Today he was but 32

No bluer eyes would compromise

His life would laugh and bring him joy

As if to say make hail old boy

The mid years were the kindest yet

and still he was able to reflect

On Love and kids and friends galore

A raucous family clan and more

A wife that his good life did serve

A mate and partner who would never swerve

Blessed with health and untold wealth

The decades did decree

That one so generous had served his world

His memory rich would be

14

MARI DILLARD

A fortunate circumstance in fate

Lead a woman to this shore

Commitment was her hardware

Friendship at her core

Filipino Culture danced within her glowing gaze

A Leader with a heart of gold

Would step up and be brave

Against the odds of life she walked

Her dignity not unscathed

She stands for all that's true and good

For people seldom know

The sacrifice of love is she

Our privilege to behold

15

IRA WILL INSPIRE YA

Ira will inspire ya

He'll bring out the fire in ya

His rap is so bad

You'll never be sad

Give it some thought

His words are more than talk

Advice for the mighty

Protection from the flighty

His wisdom will serve ya

So your life will deserve ya

Just put on his music

And dance to the beats

Sing out your story

And sus out your glory

Yea - Ira will inspire ya

16

LIZA

If the woman is invincible

Name her Liza

If she is wise powerful indestructible kind and funny

Name her Liza

Short in height tall in stature

Tiny build giant presence

Epitome of femininity

Fights for freedom

Beaten, cheated, political refugee

Afghani treasure

She walked into the unknown

Name her Liza

Daughter of the poet, married into madness, she sleeps alone

Worthy of everything, needing nothing, her style couture

Name her Liza

17

BALANCE

Within to Without

Void to Matter

Spirit to Action

Love to Lover

Am I

18

BLUE

Deep pools of blue beckon

I dive

Soft and warm

Sustaining like honey

Reassures my risk

Peering into my heart

Captured a perfect moment

19

LOVE

Infinitely indefinable

Contained in all

Subject to nothing

Subtracted from zero

Equals infinity

Tossed into the great mystery

We breeze into its mist

Fragile

Enchanted

We pray for courage to endure

Ecstasy

Just once more

20

CIRCLE OF LOVE

Ever seeking the eternal dawn

She spins into his light

Warming her body, nurturing her soul

She spins deeper....into his light

Melodic moon reflections witness

Joy in orbit

Exploring the cosmos

Stars sing

21

LOVER

Sway me with sensual softness

Shower me with your treasure

Offer me honesty

Marginalize defects

Disregard the dents

Forget the date

Volunteer truth

Receive

Boundless trust

Infinite freedom

Expanding Intimacy

Uncompromised Care

Eternal love

I will even wear pearls

22

FLY PRIVATE

Stay warm my love

Stay dry

Stay strong my love

Don't rely

On anything less

Than your own inner guide

To keep you in safety

That soon may you fly

Straight to the heart

Of my deep endless sigh…

23

SONG OF LOVE

Far away fantasies
Glide over rough terrain
In succulent silence
We purify pain

Fly with me darling
Seasons will sigh
Heavens will open
Fortunes belie

Frightened of falling
Scared of the sky
Timid of treason
Freedom's lost cry

Cast as your lover
Your smile my muse
Historical chronicle
Do not confuse

Brilliant horizons
A fresh circumstance
Listen for harmony
As light circles dance

24

TRUTH

Marry me

Travel to the end

Winter with snow

Summer with sand

Fall with abandon

Spring into dew

But never leave me

25

SACRED SEX

In its absence

Mergers litigate

Trials linger

Sensibilities are denied

Caustic remorse renews

Cynics remain envious cynics

Begging the question

Why compromise

Lovers protect one another

Loves music harmonizes hearts

Purity becomes us

Honor defines us

Captivated we mingle with the muse

Poetry trumps

Enchanted lovers

One with the Universe

Know bliss

No substitute exists

26

WARRIOR FOR LIFE

Let me soften your hardened brow

Cool the fortress within you now

Melt the barricade

Drug the guard

Strike the tirade

Bury the shroud

Wander the meadow inside your heart

Linger long in a scented breeze

Dine on loves banquet, land on your knees

Life isn't worthy unless you receive

Skies aren't blue, unless you believe

27

ELECTRIC FENCE

Ouch

Invisible

Indiscernible

Undisclosed

Conflicting

Divisive

Isolating

28

TWO HOUR TRYST

I tire of the two hour tryst

All ebb, deny the flow

A manic episodic show

A metronome inside my soul

Ticked away in time

Once waiting for the wind to shift

I thought of you as mine

29

REJECTION

Never personal

30

SUNSET

Warm glow gives way

Shine has moved on

Darkness grows reckless in the abandoned space

The edge between then and now blurs

31

CENTERFOLD

Objectify a beauty
View, a telescope's long eye
Metallic glass, massive cost
Captive, yet divine

Paid by the hour
Cast to shape commercial thought
She leaves a trace of innocence
Intact, enraged, unsought

Never mind his emptiness
Within is now without
Disregard his loneliness
His heart must figure it out

32

FAULT LINE

My love is thirsty
My heart is bereft
Sanctimonious sanctuary
Is all that is left

Walls hung with plaster
Floors lined with trees
Ceilings cloud memories
Fissure wide as seas

33

SKID ROW

It is a dying model

Man inside bottle

Poking out about the head

Diving down to check if dead

If from within the dude does spin

I'm tantamount to tantrum

Let's play what say

The scene round here is blue

But oh morose declined the toast

Made rein this rising sky

34

PINK

Relaxing within a vast bubble gum wrapper

Stunning to chew

Expansive, pops to infinite delight

Got monotonous

Sweetness spent

Time to spit it out

35

IN ANOTHER LIFETIME

We are but a fraction
Full of love but out of rhyme
Restless, ruthless, rhythms
Run against the party line
Linear light bruised warrior
Anything but sublime
Crumbs of wasted wonder
Wither a waiter's petulant whine
Whatever; let the nectar breathe - evaporates in time
Burdened by the breath of love
Merlot shrinks on the vine
Vintage wine yet dusky
Demeaning, yet we dine
Do you know the secret
Scented in the sand
Souls to love each other
On an ever distant land
Late of date yet worthy
Wandering in our wake
Winding through the heavens
Heading for our fate

36

TRANSITORY SUN

I am not your lover

I am not the one

To abandon, betray or lie too

In service of your sun

Another provisional Miss

Must serve your temporary bliss

For I am not your lover

I am not the one

I am not available

To cool your burning sun

Despite my charmed sweet fragrance

No passive nature here

Will serve ignoble appetite

Absorb your empty juice

Cry your silent tears

Hide your dreadful truth

37

TRADITIONAL FEARS

In a sea of tranquility

Rock solid regret

Stubbornly summoned it forms discontent

Past without prejudice

Futures milieu

Perjures the prayer

If only we knew

Move without motion

Cry without tears

Age although ageless

Traditional fears

38

PROMISE

To be your friend

Is all I ask

Aligned in force

Guide our course

Witness the rise

Decry the stall

Sacred heart

Throughout it all

However small

Not as lover

Not as mate

Never leave you

Never forsake

39

STARLIGHT

My father is dying
I'm watching him go
His soul is withdrawing
To where I don't know

I cannot stop the pace of life
Dam up its ebb and flow
Nature's endless rhapsody
Conspires to let us go

Enraptured by simplicity
Confined to R an R
My spirit overwhelmed with grief
Grateful to a star

40

DEATH

Evidence of life

Evidence of love

Evidence of joy

Evidence of loss

Evidence of transformation

Evidence of Life

41

A BLUEBIRD floats down from unseen nest

And lit upon my grieving breast

Burrows deep within my heart

Lays an egg in haste - departs

I'm stunned, in turmoil, the blessed thing

To distracted to sense the season is spring

I am transfixed, my paradigm split, for now my heart must settle

To nurture harmony I pay the price for my innocent tenant's

gestation

Need I be peaceful, need I be still, and need I forget my conundrum

To secure the scene, ensure the life and forget my own distraction

I guess I can drop my drama for now, delay grief's resurrection

My ruined countenance I must set aside, a truer virtue let shine

By and by my heart grows soft, attunes to an innocent beat

Soon it's followed by cracking shell; a chirp announces its leap

I catch the chick as it dives into life for now I am the net

And set it back within my heart certain its time is nigh

Who will I be next my heart disagrees

My little charge confides

"Am I to be your reminder

You will be who you are

I, never far

You, ever the chooser"

…..

42

REPOSE

Stunning stillness

Witness

Remember

Internalize

Sleep

43

SYNERGY

Footfalls

Never reveal her intention

To witness her was enough

Aloof to the patterns of commerce

Akin to the melody of life

She journeys

Lifted by harmony

Magic became destiny

44

EDGES

Walk softly the edge of life

Where searing sunsets meet cool dawn and

Life's infinite circles pair magic with song

Faded rays of fragrant light seal a promise and a fate

Amethyst passions unlock her fragile chamber gate

Bouquet to spark warm embers charm

A waning bleak heart rate

Promised faded dreams of old

Long forgotten over winter's cold

Regenerate in cinders fold

No matter the content the scenes all fulfill

Remind me to travel no paths ever still

Pain's only beautiful if turned off at will

Wander ancient gardens taste a wise vine

Deepen its clarity if plucked in good time

Lavender circles blush soft purple wine

45

JOURNEY

If fortune favors the bold my friend

This journey was long foretold

Erratic scenes carve fateful myth

In turbulent transformational triumphant glyph

Riveting rivers tripped the gates to passion's reign of flame

Concentric circles converge mid stream, sanguine to the sea

Steam exploded at storm's behest

And life gave reign to me

Basking in starlight and roiling in foam

Secured my freedom once more

A wizened voice on the wind once hummed

a prophet's poignant song

All roads lead to another my dear this journey is no end

Dreams of today oft spoken for will surely come round again

Now I rest at my Soul's behest

On cumulus clouds of change

Content with life's eternal entreat

The key to be

Is thee

46

WISDOM OF AIRE

An effervescent breeze renews

Effulgent mythic blaze infused

It lights the stream where flows my life

In silhouette, thick haze I muse

Stay the course sweet breath decries

As stars caress my sultry eyes

Sail I on - ask I ~ a faint whisper guides my cue

Within these sparkling bubbles lies a message, ere a clue

Rich memories of the chapter next are known to be quite true

Remember wherein your heart sang free

Sense its beat, sail on

When next you lay your anchor down

Upon a hallow shore

Spin a sacred web for two

We will chant the lore

47

SOUL OF A WOMAN

Inward passage to outward lie
Worlds within world's bygone futures spy

Spirals within plumb our depths and spin
We plan and we act till our dreams come in

Limitless thoughts fire a passionate life
We birth a world sensitive to strife

When it blooms we delight, when it dies we retreat
To replant or rebirth, we know not defeat

We dream for peace, we dream children survive
We dream of balance, we dream all life will thrive

We act from our hearts, we act for the truth
Gaining strength from loves eternal youth

When we understand peace
Our Souls will release

A creative referral of
Universal renewal

Journey in Life

48

LIFE

Drifting toward endless skies sail I

Beyond the Southern Cross

Will brilliance light the vast expanse

Steady my stern and guide my course

Away, before my plan is hatched

I journey forth on grace and creed

To sow the existential seed

49

O

Mystery charms old Owl tonight

She calls from the tree of life

Her candor irrefutable

Her manner never trite

Whatever be her nature

Need never be concealed

Truth can hold no prisoner

All will be revealed

Perception navigates far and near

Late breezes sculpt my listening ear

Rapturous wisdom ensues

For better or worse I pursue my muse

Lay her voice into meter

Deliver in verse

A rhyme with true cadence

Just and diverse

50

A COSMIC INVITATION

Ether beckons stars, arise
A moons advice lifts the tides
Breezes swing under wings that glide
Sparks liberate flames far and wide

Wonder elicits a wandering eye
Mystery sweetens the view
Magical myth in melodic verse
Life itself will pursue

Come to me when you are thirsty
Come to me if you are blind
Come, take the keys to the cosmos
Come and inspire your mind

51

SPACE

Open the night

Trillions of eyes foresee each dawn

Ever pulsing

The cosmos like lava smolders

On and on and on

We fly within

Lifted into the abyss

Suns explode

Stars

Never denied life

Unite

52

STARS

Speckle darkened dunes

Sense their twinkling song

Weave them into tapestry

Wrap them in ribbons

Place them with care

Into darkness

53

SUN

Heart of all being

Surround the senses

Mesmerizing fire

Gaseous arches

In spiral sparkling sanctuaries

We burn

Emblazoned in linear light

Formed for timeless travel

Incinerated

We merge

Into Love

54

BIOLOGY FOR THE UNBORN

Silently sitting above the great shore

Rolling crescendos conduct torrid roar

Blind to the view

Eyes already knew

This pristine expanse

Is only a clue

55

SEED FOR A PERFECT 5TH

Dark cosmos shimmers within a captive dream

Frolic ferments loam while seasons redeem

Fire kisses ice births rain and steam

Droplets form a delicate stream

Tensions entice a moonlit foray

Sown seedlings surrender their song be gay

Harmony sounds amidst the humus and fray

Forgetful fruit foretell full harvest day

A delicate key is struck

Coded to grow

Enchanted gardens

Glow

56

GARDEN AT GLENDALOUGH

Silent secrets charge the aire

Rippling rhythms graze the lair

Grass and trees long fingertips

Beckon breezes kiss wee lips

Who can hear the deeper sigh

Buried within a falcon's cry

Her reflective refrain lingers high ore

Soaring cliffs and ponds that lie

Over yon mist on Glendalough high

Twinkling tunes fill fragrant aire

Sprinkle dew on fairies' hair

Seekers marvel of magic's flare

Sacred songs soothe ageless fare

Darkest winds proclaim and dare

Soothe your soul in natures lair

Mysteries deep await you there

57

SEA OF DREAMS

Aspire ye of little faith

False prophet's charge while centuries forsake

Forgotten dreams swirl, foam and curl

Roar the gait as futures unfurl

Trust its author's salty spray

Will take us deeper day by day

True, wind and wild the tides reflect

Though tempests linger shadows protect

Complete the life with sweet sublime

To tarry will but shrink the rhyme

58

CONSTANCE

The crew had surmised

No passenger deduced

The path to destruction

Would fail to reduce

Eschew its merit to balance the chart

Failing delivery beyond the rampart

Marred without misery

Plagued with no doubt

Moving with majesty too oft to count

Frequently flying under the gun

Sailing on energy spent by the sun

Was it the map on an ancient whale's tooth

That led to dead reckoning - a mariner's truth

59

A WILLOWS SYMPHONY

A sky song wept a symphony

Silence between each drop

Swills and swells cacophony

Music never stops

Surrenders every single note

Cherish all will be

Weep away oh willow

Sway beneath the sea

Past became what once was dawn

Like circles in the sand

Do not fret I'll care for you

Till harmony fills the land

60

POETS

Poets are passionately narrative of life
Though some be stuck
On cave dwelling antic dotes
Sexually plucked

We design our deep thoughts
To appear into sight
A sense of adventure
To quicken our plight

Aren't we endlessly
Weighing the line
To bring up a heavy
Throwing back slime

Peacefully caught up
In participle space
While nixing an article
Placing an i into case

For those of us blessed
With the will and the way
We weave weary rhetoric
Into nuance and fray

Will our merits be noted
Our failures denied
So poets may freely
Wander tween lines

To gift you with patterns
So dear to your heart
The willing will perish
The stoic will not

61

SUBURBIA

The suburbs almost killed me

Trapped in concrete and endless repetition

Escape was futile

Numb it down

Find meaning in a key

For everything is locked

62

SQUEEZING LIMES

I was a pirate

A seeker of song

Secretly downloading

Was I really wrong

My studio is silent

My muse is asleep

My iPod went missing

Limewire was cheap

I never burned one

Just listened to fav's

Both Leonard and Bernie

Inspired this naive

A little tune with sentiment

Poetic meter with rhyme

Music inspires me

What is my fine

63

THEATRE SURREAL

Gleaming glass tile

Red blazing walls

Orbiting stage now in view

Hastens us back to our pew

Fiery comets sail the wind

Dip dry lips into dew

Echo sings of purplish hail

Private attire never knew

Steal the stage from the theatre

Disperse the cast far and near

Curtail critic affidavit

Obscure the witless review

64

ADDICTION

Parasitic energies stalk humanity's brilliant

A seductive lover's entreat

Wounded innocence their entrée

Deluded illusion, the defeat

Ravenous for the juice

Life force is stolen

Resolves fade to futility

Shamed and enslaved

We weep

Till

The will of love awakens

Purification sanctifies souls

Truth replaces the lie

Compassion makes us whole

Power claimed victory

As addictions die to dust

Life calls forth our service

Enlightened, we finally trust

65

DESPERATION

Surfaces look tranquil

Lifestyle pushing on

Blazing forth horizons

No love, career, forgone

Enter vast reversal

Catastrophic angst

Flooding waters waver forth

Foundations footings fail

How to cope

Cascading moat

Desperate for compassion

My psyches in refraction

66

WAR

Forged in the fountain of hardship

Hung in the annals of time

Twisted around aristocracies

Artfully towing the line

Littered with portraits of patriots

Patiently plying their trade

Training the next generation

Gratefully young and afraid

67

RELIGION

Uses of honoring God

Divisive conviction breeds fear

Dogmatic rhetoric controls

Hypocritical positional superiority, directs policy

Uses of honoring God

Unrepentant warring

Religious murder accepted

Commercially marketed the faithless expand

Uses of honoring God

Incorrigible subjugation of children

Human trafficking

Denied, hidden, acknowledged, tolerated

Uses of honoring God

Serve humanity

Love and wisdom

Intelligence as light

68

NAMELESS MEN

Angry man is unoriginal

Angry man can't create

Angry man is insular

Angry man won't partake

Angry man will pollute

Angry man will forsake

Angry man sees no solution

To angry man's lost evolution

Angry man will destroy every harmony

Angry men could possess

Angry men create strife

Then angry men blame life

Angry men only use

Then angry men abuse

Angry men honor the warrior

Angry men fight for peace

Angry men distain unity

Lost, they ferment

Angry man must repent

69

ANOTHER SMALL WOMAN'S LIFE UNDONE

Politician power's priestly prose
Repeated history, since God only knows
Train those boys, follow the leader
Do what you're told, or live in the cold

Go to war, dominate the score
Control your market, lies your tool
Blind as bats, they learn it in school
Honesty to them, the mark of a fool

Plug your socket in a brothel
Reap your reward
Rape and run
Too much fun

Where it leads, destructions feed
Sick entertainments prophetic deed
Media fed monopoly, no real heart
Blurs the line between profit and art

Fact or fiction, ratings soar
Hype engendered, stokes their member
Governing losers, talk pure smack
Inconsequential queries, don't talk back

Hide in power, run amok
Moneyed men, bought the moxy
Privileged addiction, premeditated thug
Defend insanity, score the drug

THE ROOSTER

Fire bites his feathered flounce
Furnace flames his face
Foreign to his feathers
Fruit of loin, doeth ever shake

Sensitive to no-one
Sensual while sedate
Signs away his solace
Seals away his fate

Fugitive or fears remain
Frigid folly's old domain
Passed within forgotten fruit
Live seeds that never die

When the seasons ripen
When nature links with time
Will I know this pathway
Wind and sand hath smoothed behind

Will I know it by its view
Or smell, or taste, or vine
I'll know it by its harmony
If only I find mine

71

MOMENTS

Moments flicker their memories fade

The stuff of dreams its endless cascade

Forever we choose summon heartache and bliss

Determine a path to ensure we exist

Oblivion merits a story charade

Schooled definition falls short, leaves a haze

Religious encryption, controlling the maze

72

KNOW

She said "Forgive them"

I said "Whatever"

She said "They made you strong"

I said "They made me defiant"

A world hostile to woman births another baby girl

Savage suffocation is welcome to unfurl

Flip the hostile highway carve truth into the curb

Balance and empower woman

Birth a sacred fearless world

Did I forgive them

Of course, you knew I might

How else would I ever know

Which role in life was right

73

TSUNAMI

Oceans of emotions

Tsunamis of tide

Wrinkles on the brow line

Do less than provide

Irony sweeps up the streets

Trims the vine,

Silently satin,

It weaves the next line

Am I a prisoner or am I on leave

Is my tour of duty, any time now relieved

The venture's been virtuous

It's imperfectly true

Render me tranquil

Render me new

74

THE ARRANGEMENT

As I gaze beyond a deep blue sky

Into futures wherein my life will fly

And wonder a dream for slaves as I

Would free our shackled souls, untie?

Or does the slave within my mind

Unfold at will my life's design

Beckon to God for freedoms code

To prove a Jew's lost legacy, foretold

And by and by our trust restores

Unwitting slaves confined no more

75

GRIEVING

Stalls before the twist

Over time and in its time

Language reverts to mist

Sensible explanations lose their rhythm and their rhyme

Knees collapse the scene goes din, surreal yet sharp defined

Shatter all the current plans, revert into a cave

Await an explanation for this uncanny painful haze

Fogs lift off eventually, suspicions unconfirmed

Challenged aire was hailing, searing ice singe strength infirm

Let it pass, don't take it on, let wisdom test the veil

The result set is disputable, just open up and sail

Yesterday's tomorrow is today's moment of truth

Love and sorrow both remain, an enigma is turned loose

In my mind it's certain, in my heart its pain

In my soul it's wiser, to dance into the rain

76

DECONSTRUCTION

Drop the baggage

Lose certainty

Forget what's known

Past drift off

Horizon expand

Sacred structured

Magic enters

Meridians of intention meet

Metrics fail

Science stalled

Stones smile

Life renewed

SPIRITUALITY

If ever I wonder if God is alive

Turn off my eyes

That I might witness the memory of beauty

And forget the color of the sky

If ever I stand in denial of the endless life of my soul

Turn off my mind

That I might witness the memory of darkness

And forget all intuition

If ever I wonder if love is immortal

Turn off my heart

That I might witness the memory of my loves

And forget the magic of their embrace

If ever I wonder

Life would be empty

My spirit enslaved

78

SAFFRON SAIL

My dream is to float cheek to cheek with a cloud

Rise on a thermal sleek as a breeze

Float through the future

Spy past with great ease

Silently lifting as light corners dark

Briskly surpassing the moments next mark

Nothing can touch me, freedoms prevail

Wind is my master, saffron my sail

79

INTUITION

Observation profoundly charged

Over arching impressions emerge

New common denominators form

Let go

A channel opens

Dimensions of thought broaden in scope

Observe

Relieved

Intuition circles within

80

SIMPLICITY

Elegant

Humble

Uncertain

Practical

Peaceful

Expansive

Honest

Brilliant

Perfect

81

IMAGINATION

Is she ever whimsical

Life storms sweep my inner landscape

In the mist she disappears

From whence will she emerge

Through endless tedious years

How to sustain

Simply

Trust

Yourself

She says

Play

82

LABYRINTH

When truth about truth is timeless
And time within time takes flight
Circles within circles will be science
And lives within life will bring sight

Concealed are my Soul's deepest secrets
Etched in the stone I traverse
Standing outside orchestrating
Paths between paths lie reversed

Somewhere within I am troubled
Somewhere within I am free
Somewhere within I am reckless
Somewhere within lies the key

Summer's moon chants to the mountains
Water conspires to prance
Winter regrets fall's failures
Spring brings with her a new chance

Why does the life live us backward
Savoring youth with a glance
Driving our path ever inward
Dissolving the trek as we pass

83

THE STONES OF DUBLIN

Though slick and shiny souls belie

Stones encrusted worn and rounded corners high

From ages dark and dank they sigh

Form dreary cages marked by sages

From past ages still they lie

Live I within these heart hewn walls

Unfettered by blizzards of icy vice

Wicked warriors and tattered mice

Hold I foul memories of bygone breezes

Fraught with steamy strife

Look I upon the changing mercies

Buried within as pulsing ice

Unfettered crevice conceals visions

Flanked by cobblestones buried thrice

Know I, an Irish ballad haunting

Stones did witness its twinkling gleam

To melt the myth and reawaken

Our daunting, ever present Irish dream

84

PHOENIX

Shining through ashes

Rising in flashes

Phonetically phrasing mythology at will

The idea is ludicrous

It merits no pun

It's burning in paradise whatever from

The stark realization that the exit is up

Lightness of being must empty its cup

So what of the view from the height of the soar

If only a myth

Then whatever for

85

EARTH SPEAK

Humanity – a word please

Self destruction on myriad levels

Necessitates intervention

Witness

Nature reorganizing

Every breath you take is and has always been

At our discretion

Every thought you think, every word you speak

Appears within our collective mind

Devastated paradise

Reflects your depth of thought and action

Iroquois wisdom sustains

Until evident

Cherish each privileged moment

86

JAPANESE SACRIFICE

Fire above us

Fire aglow

Fire within us

Fire below

Wander, witness, withdraw, recant

Waters steamy mirage, revamp

Irradiant message in fission flows

If Humans tread where the sun never goes

Broad is our territory, vast are our gifts

Boundaries protect to ensure we exist

Scorched resurrection, baptism by fire

Sum of our senses will quicken, inspire

The world understands now

The depth of your soul

Heart of a people

Hidden no more

87

ACID RAIN

Observe the endless human race

Tumbling forth through vigilant space

Circular tracks

Always takes us back

Karmas prophetic fact

Prose and penalties persist

Sculpting consciousness within we exist

Wyle away the hours

Dreaming for a life

Brimming with purpose

Devoid of strife, while

Stoic sarcophagus hails

A silent storm

Clear acid rain

Converts succulent norm

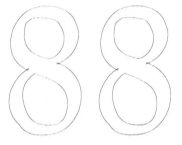

BANQUET FOR A WAKE

Rage whips up a fiery froth

Rape will crack the sea

Toxins churn a rhapsody

Leaders can't foresee

Abandoned babies

Cry all night

For love has ceased to be

Children hungry bought and sold

Schools shut down en masse

Plea for future sake

Spirit don't forsake

Ignorant of power

Lunacy we make

Sup a meager antidote

Banquet for a wake

89

EDUCATION

Absent from class

Empowerment

Harmlessness

Inclusiveness

Creativity

Diversity

Respect

Mystery

Culture

Truth

Art

Future Proof Life

90

I'M QUALIFIED

I'm qualified

For this job and that

I'm over qualified to wear this hat

I'd be qualified wherever I sat

Memorize that

Play the fool

Show up to school

The burden's on you

You could even drool

And you could be qualified

Want a degree to make me free

Qualified to know 'what is a tree'

Treat me to secrets that control the wind

Bring me a blanket, make sure it's skin

Fry me a steak, make sure I win

So stuck in qualified

Stuck in so smart

Deeply stuck,

In the dark

91

HAITI

An ancient African mist foretold

Where Human hearts bought and sold

A quake would brew an intervention bold

Then wind would right wrong use of psalms

Fleece forever greasy palms

Restitution necessitates, heed its beckon call

On a fractured Caribbean island karma would forestall

Generations left behind by worlds of time and greed

Sanctuaries soul surrounds solitude and need

Thousands of generous hearts did heed

Mercy merits no introduction, warm hand

Grievous suffering on blood stained land

Distracted world prevailed, then ran

Attention reallocated, on demand

Promises broken, by command

Children of Haiti

Forgive Us

92

EVOLUTION

Stars do it

Butterflies do it

Humanity a wash in process

Alone yet together

Scheduled for rebirth

As blessed

Benefactors

93

PHOENIX - AZ

Town with a game to big to tame

A mythic bird even bore its name

Not by parent

Not by blame

Charged with a task to big to ask

Rise from your ashes

Not by flask

Not by fame

Soar city soar

Source your destiny from fires core

Native mazes

Sought by sages

Bought in stages

Sun lit pages

Golden ages

94

COURAGE

Rite of passage

Earned by few, staged by many

Rewarded rarely

It listens

Considers consequences

True to truth

Selfless

Suffers in silence

Owns the future

Leads

95

RE-INCARNATION

Genius delivered by protégé
Nature's comedic debut
Character's integral from birth
Deliver knowledge and wisdom, on que
Each child a summation of their unique lives
Brilliant virtues influence generations of vice
Impacting community with inspired life
Together we travel the spiral
Circle the labyrinth renewed
Gift our light to the sacred center
Sustained by the love we ensue

While

Warriors resolve to war
Addictions dominate the ignorant
Funding greed's territorial score
Death penalties perjure the sane
Criminal's reborn recriminate
Karma's endless refrain
Lost, we circle the labyrinth
Dread our perilous fate
Project the ultimate illusion
Encounter our power
Too late

96

WIND

Commissioned by spirit

Landscapes shift

Ideas blow by

Humanity sniffs

Cocoons in plastic

Ice melts

Messages dangle in drops

Mirth merges into an oily glob

Craters open

Slim falls in

Humanity

Saved again

By wind

97

FREEDOM

Lost in combat

Struck down in court

Isolated

Layered between concrete block

Smothered at birth

Reborn each moment

Preserved in art

Frozen in time

As constant as the sea

As unforgettable as a kiss

Reborn each moment

Forever

Will prevail

98

I AM MIGRATION
YO SOY MIGRANTE

Life
Vida

Travel as water
Viajando como el agua

Alive when flowing
Viva cuando fluye

Rancid if stagnant
Rancio si se estanca

Indigenous birthright
Indigena de Nacimiento

Enchanted Earth
Tierra encantada

Reflect our dream
Refleja nuestros sueños

Open borders
Fronteras abiertas

Steward everything
Cuidador de todo

Protect life
Protejo la vida

Treasure children
Valora los *niños*

Grateful for each breath we borrow
Agradecidos por cada respiro que tomamos prestado

99

THE NETWORK

Gossamer

Electric threads

Lay lines of silken thought

Heartwarming storms of change

Evolve

We whisper

Touch one another

Subtle

Gentle

Provocative

Visceral transmissions pulse

Until then

Hardwire

100

FUTURE PROOF

The wind is still

The drops don't invade

My balcony beckons

Life's stormy charade

Yet I am ensconced

In the worlds I create

Peacefully musing

Mysteries next gate

I wander the sunset

Dive into the deep

Carve resurrection

Till my life is complete

Babies are anxious

Mothers asleep

Children predict which fortunes will peak

Generations of healers will transform our fate

Forgive us our folly

Understand what's at stake

101

ANCESTORS

Legacy of ages

Blood lines mix

Impressions stir

Nature organizes lives

Dreams re-awaken

Failed possibilities prevail

Awareness creates power

Wisdom sustains

No effort

No dream

No love

Lost

102

ABUNDANCE

Starved of affection

Under realized

Shamed into an apology

Fictionalized into an art form

Mocked by the masses

We retreat to what we know

Suffering greed

Until

We strike the corded wellspring of denial

Stunned

Sustained

We are made whole

Every eternal moment festooned in blazing possibility

Elemental

Guaranteed

103

HUMAN NATURE

Mysterious space

Particulate light

Manifest universe

Creative insight

Celestial treasure map

Secrets of life

A dimensional language

In Cosmic code

Grasp its sequence

Unlocked, as foretold

Awe in awareness

Align into sight

Realize magic

Soar into light

104

CHERISH THE SEASON

Cherish the season
Let merry your soul
Link with another
Let love's flicker soar

One candle binds us
Seven surround
Eight lead us forward
Into the sound

Sing of creation
Hymn to God's grace
Vision renewal
For the whole Human race

Why am I doubtful
Why do I fret
Trust without merit
Ends me in debt

Step into dreamscape
I'll hold your hand
My Fairies and Angels
Hold court in this land

Images melt into rainbows of sand
Dew drops contain every spice I command
Magic ever the breeze under foot
Sets life in motion o'er every ocean

105

UNITY

Coalesced before time

Devoid of space

Unilateral

Spawning diversity

Defines the matrix

Ubiquitous

Stunningly prosperous

Frighteningly powerful

Our destiny to manifest

Key to survival

Omnipotent

Divine

106

FACING THE SKY

Alone in the cosmos are we
Silence pervades a moon lit haze
Still somewhere within
Skies open up and welcome us in

Facing the Sky
A singular song
Prances on water and beckons us on
Break with tradition to the future you belong

Witness its dignity
A face with no name
Calling us forward
To dance and proclaim

Struck by its majesty
A symphony explodes
Breathtaking truth
The measure of prose

The sea is your mother
The wind is your tide
The Fire within you
Will never subside

The face of forever
Spirit of life
Signals anew
Arts eternal milieu

107

IF LIGHT WERE FORGIVING

Apocalyptic sentiments soar

Through ancient tales we hear their roar

Humanity lost its divine entreat

If Light were forgiving

It would not retreat

Creative intervention evens the score

Humanity refreshed, sustains once more

Till the ignorant urge demeans our core

And Earth postures a structured uproar

If Light were forgiving

It would not retreat

But merit the method and shine forth a sign

Signaling us onward, Light wanders sublime

Challenging our favor, stating a fact

Since Light is forgiving

Our future's in tact

108

POWER

Silence

Bear witness

Lightness in motion

Will span every ocean

Compassionate patience sustains

Heart drives the motive

Intentions are clear

A light in the darkness will always appear

Our transforming nature made clear

Roll back the rhetoric

Shut down the insane

Ego maniacal formats contain

Power mixed in the ether take rein

Human conditions expand and sustain

109

MEDICINE FOR MADNESS

Molecules multiply, if muted they morn

Musty morning musings, mutate a fierce storm

Mind filled with madness, pursues dark terrain

Weakened by folly, demand a refrain

Beauty and truth illumine the dream

Light informs art and refreshes the stream

Art is the vision

Art is the heart

Art is the medicine

That breaches the dark

110

A GLOBAL AWAKENING

Astonishing futures beckon
Ancient paradigms inspire
Quantum dynamics clue innovative resolutions
If sustainable systems fulfill their destiny

Partnership charts our course
Transparency insures democracy
Collaboration defines development
Tapestries of hope illumine the way

Empowered woman
Liberate the spirit of life on earth
Prepare for collective rebirth
Principled milieu triumphant

Educated children enrich cultural nations
Creating a renaissance of innovation
Health guides lives of service
Economics dichotomous purpose

When sustainable systems fulfill their destiny
Peace
Governs
Life

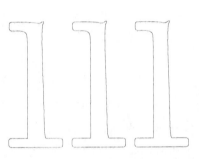

FUTURE

Through the ages

Masters of worlds within worlds lit our way

Creative wisdom

Sustained

Celestial light birthed splendor

Earth renewed

Our beautiful pain filled journey

As reckless as it will seem in retrospect

Delivered universal truth when

All

Life

Knew

Itself

As

Sacred

About the Author

From diverse roots spring poetry. Powerful, insightful, wise, piercing metaphors infuse her work. Her poetic expression exposes issues with authentic clarity. This work expresses not only personal sensibilities, but is directed more fundamentally to inspire creation of paradigm shifting possibilities for her global family.

Her poetry, often performed with musicians, takes her to Dublin, Ireland where she's warmly received at *Glór Sessions*, Tongue Box and The Library; in Phoenix and Southern California from San Diego to LA.

The poem "I AM Migration" offers a provocative immigration commentary with global implications. As a former labor organizer this issue struck a chord and Parsons has responded with poetic resonance.

Her poem *"Japanese Sacrifice"* produced as a video interpretation is viewable on You Tube in multiple languages. This poem expresses the tragedy facing Japan and the global lesson their national sacrifice demands, the end of nuclear fission.

Pursuing a passion for journalism Holly has held several editorial positions in the states and overseas and is an independent contributor and ardent supporter of transparency in journalism. Privately, she supports cultural awareness as the way to global peace through her non-profit work.

Early in life, a commitment to supporting equality and human dignity consistently define her life choices. Conventional social norms if divisive, exclusive or demeaning discover here an articulate activist. *Parsons pen is poised and prolific.*

Her deeper interests remain with social justice, philosophy, cultural anthropology, Zen Buddhism, Taoism, Kabbalah and Ageless Wisdom Teaching.

Her recent poem *"Global Awakenings"* commissioned by the 28 year non-profit Global Interactions for *The World Academy for the Future of Woman* to focus the UN Millennium Development Goals, is featured on numerous corporate and non-profit websites.

Holly's poem commemorating the legendary life of acting educator, Deirdre O'Connell hangs in Dublin's Focus Theatre. The historic *"Winding Stair"* bookstore in Dublin, Ireland honored her with shelving her first Limited Edition collection *"Spring Journey, Footsteps for Love and Life"* and *"Soul of A Woman."* Her next collection of poems and a series of children's poetry books are in development.

Born in *Syracuse,* NY, of Irish, English, Middle Eastern and Russian cultures; she is the mother of two artists, and grandmother of three glorious girls. Holly currently resides in the high desert of Arizona.

www.HollyParsons.com

Commentary on Selected Poems

1   THE MAIDEN
My 20th high school reunion inspired this poem. Memories of our bond, innocence and youth granted me once again, an overwhelming sense of camaraderie with a hundred young women.

4   MOTHERHOOD
I found myself in love with a man of color and pregnant at 18. Alone and ostracized, I was relegated to social outcast - overnight. The prospect of motherhood terrifying - this poem describes my journey through and out the other side.

5   HOPE
My son's name was chosen by his father because "That's all I have to give him." Now a man, he recently commented "Mum, you know it's hard to be depressed about anything for more than an hour when your name is Hope." The name proved to be enough.

6   DAUGHTERS
Graced with a daughter of immeasurable grace and presence since birth...I was once again blessed by motherhood.

10   SPICE OF LIFE
Written after helping my daughter settle her family into a new home, overcome with the cycles and possibilities for both her life and my granddaughters.

11   MRS E
This extraordinary woman and I became friends in 1970, she 43 and I 17. Kindred spirits, she understood my soul, gave me a home when I needed one, supported a new mother's fears and has remained a rock in my life for upwards of 40 years.

12   DEIRDRE O'CONNELL

I was invited to write this posthumous tribute to the legendary Deirdre O'Connell, who taught method acting for 36 years in Dublin Ireland. My son was her student for the last 3 years of her life. In homage I read to the acting community gathered for a screening of the documentary of her life, at the International Film Institute in Dublin in 2010. It was the first time I'd ever read one of my poems.

13   CODY

My son in law, friend and great man, who does his level best and does it well!

14   MARI DILLARD

Mari presides over the Asian American Association in Arizona which distinguishes itself by honoring the Cultures of Asia without regard to national lines of demarcation or religion. She stands for diversity and unity in the Arizona desert.

15   IRA WILL INSPIRE YA

Ira Weitz, circa NYC, this Bronx educator and guidance counselor, performed his inspired rap written for children 6 -11 years of age at an open mike event in Cave Creek, AZ. His gift for virtuous verse knocked me out!

16   LIZA

My personal friendship with a political refugee from Afghanistan, one of the most exceptional people I have ever known, is a treasure in my life.

37   TRADITIONAL FEARS

Love endures through every season, beyond reason.

41   BLUEBIRD
At one point I realized seven of my friends [including myself] were dealing with loss and grief. At that moment I observe, "A Bluebird floats down from unseen nest..."

49   O
A humble tribute to my feathered friends haunting hoot, her inspiration in the wee hours of the night: my muse.

54   BIOLOGY FOR THE UNBORN
Sitting on the roof of the Glider Port atop the cliff's north of La Jolla, a group of professors and I traded speculations on life...and this poem was born.

55   SEED FOR A PERFECT 5TH
My friend Harold Moses and I planted a huge summer garden - no small feat in Arizona. His inspired piano scores played to our gardens delight and we were blessed by an abundant yield beyond our wildest expectations.

56   GARDEN AT GLENDALOUGH
This poem was written while lazing in long grass at the Glendalough nature preserve in Ireland. Absorbing the ambiance and watching shadows reflect my son and granddaughter vamping in the sparkling lake at sunset.

58   CONSTANCE
Intuition, a fail-safe guide when ancient maps go awry.

62   SQUEEZING LIMES
When the free music service 'LimeWire' was taken off the air... over 200 of my favorite tunes instantly disappeared. I was in withdrawal for a week.

Inspired by Cirque de Soleil. All theatre no matter how perfect – is a gift to the world.

A litany of duplicity penetrates the airwaves. Betrayal infiltrates the psychology of commitment at all levels - our world demands virtuous leadership…intolerance informs this poem.

A Chinese painting of a wild-eyed rooster viewing his progeny with impatient disdain inspired this poem.

A spontaneous conversation with a friend - on a day when my edge was unraveling, prompted this conversation.

My grandmother was a Jewish refugee. Upon being invited to my first Seder - I wrote this in deference to the past and with hope for the future. One meaning of the word Seder רדסה לילל *is 'Arrangement'.*

I learned the skill of deconstruction from my granddaughter Gaia when she was 11 months old. Following her lead and deconstructing my life provided the opening through which this poetry flows.

All my life I have employed the methods described in this poem. Never considering that one day sensitivity, passion and my inquiring nature would disclose my thoughts in verse.

83   THE STONES OF DUBLIN

While walking the beautiful streets of Dublin, Ireland, my son outlined the political era leading to Irish independence from British rule. I could hear the battles and feel the pain which spanned nearly 800 years as the Irish fought off incursion after incursion... from many oppressive cultures. My ancestors escaped to America three generations ago, yet my son created his life in Dublin, and provides a measure of healing to these resilient and gifted people. Agniactingstudio.com

85   EARTH SPEAK

Until we listen and take action to restore this planet, she will continue to speak to us directly; in ways that get our attention.

86   JAPANESE SACRIFICE

I knew the morning of the quake that nuclear facilities in Japan were compromised. Ten days later, my intuition confirmed, I was invited to read this poem at a memorial service held at the Japanese Friendship Garden in Phoenix. Now viewable on YouTube, the video includes salient facts about the uncontrollable nature of nuclear fission.

91   HAITI

Clearly, we have forgotten.

98   I AM MIGRATION

Written in protest where borders control migration patterns of Human Beings to any degree on this planet [exception criminals]. I remain outraged by the cruelty and greed that lays at the core of all migration restrictions. The US and Southern states turned a blind eye on the Mexican border for a 150 years, while exploiting the impoverished people of Mexico as cheap labor. We deliberately isolated Mexico from technology advancements and denied them the benefit of education. Relegating the population to untold hardship under corrupt governments. We are the poor neighbor.

106 FACING THE SKY

"Facing the Sky" is an iconic project created by internationally celebrated visionary artist Cerj Lalonde.
The extraordinary designs evident in many of Lalonde's renderings beckon forth an appreciation for the unified essence that lies within. A mysterious image will appear on the world stage in December 2012 for a few special weeks, stay tuned Miami…

107 IF LIGHT WERE FORGIVING

A line from a poem by Jack Evans, one of Phoenix's most prolific poets, educators and organizers formed the writing prompt for a local poetry challenge… His inspiration is embedded in the sentiments swirling in my poem.

110 A GLOBAL AWAKENING

This poem was commissioned by Global Interactions for the World Academy for the Future of Women; it highlights the Millennium Development Goals required for a sustainable world.

Alphabetical Index

THE GREAT INVOCATION

From the point of light within the Mind of God
Let light stream forth into the minds of men.
Let light descend on Earth.

From the point of Love within the Heart of God
Let love stream forth into the hearts of men
May Christ return to Earth.

From the center where the Will of God is known
Let purpose guide the little wills of men -
The purpose that the Masters know and serve.

From the Center which we call the race of men
Let the Plan of Love and Light work out.
And may it seal the door where evil dwells.

Let Light and Love and Power restore the Plan on Earth

The Tibetan

9892144R0016

Made in the USA
Charleston, SC
21 October 2011